CHESS FOR KIDS

MY FIRST BOOK TO LEARN HOW TO PLAY AND WIN

YORA ROCKS

Copyright 2021 All rights reserved©.

The contents of this book may not be reproduced, duplicated or transmitted without the direct written permission of the author. Under no circumstances shall any legal responsibility or liability be imputed to the publisher for any repair, damage or monetary loss due to the information contained herein, either directly or indirectly.

Legal Notice:

No part of the contents of this book may be amended, distributed, sold, used, quoted, or paraphrased without the consent of the author.

Disclaimer Notice:

The information contained herein is for educational and entertainment purposes only. No warranties of any kind are expressed or implied. Readers acknowledge that the author is not engaged in rendering legal, financial, medical, or professional advice.

INDEX

1. PIECES

2. HOW TO MOVE THE PIECES

3. ELEMENTS

4. SPECIAL MOVES

5. SOME RULES

6. END OF GAME

Learning chess is great because:

1. **It incentivizes creativity and imagination**

It has been proven by a scientific study that by analyzing different possible plays, both of the brain hemispheres work together. These results were valid for expert players as much for amateur ones.

When thinking about possible moves, it's not just about following patterns or repeating previous plays, but evaluating the current possibilities and imagining what could happen until the end of the game.

2. Help kids to understand that their actions have consequences

There are multiple benefits from playing chess for people of all ages and <u>there are specific benefits for children</u>. One of them is that it helps them to accept rules and assuming the consequences of their actions.

It is a game where chances don't play a role. Everything is on the table in plain sight and the movements depend only on the players. There isn't an outside element that could affect the development of the game.

3. **It is entertaining and it improves your mood.**

Let's not forget that chess is still a game, so of course it has the same positive characteristics than any other game.

It is entertaining and allows you to interact with other people, no matter the age or nationality (there is no need to speak another language). You can also play from a distance using several available websites. And it is free or almost free, you just need the board and the pieces or an internet connection.

4. **It improves reading skills**

Finally, another important benefit that chess brings is that it helps children improve their reading skills. In fact, a scientific study found that students who play chess improved their reading skills much more than another group that did not participate in any chess program.

1. PIECES

- PAWN
- ROOK
- BISHOP
- KNIGHT
- QUEEN
- KING

PAWN

- **Each player has 8 pawns.**
- **They are placed on the second row.**
- **They are placed along the entire second row, as can be seen in the image.**

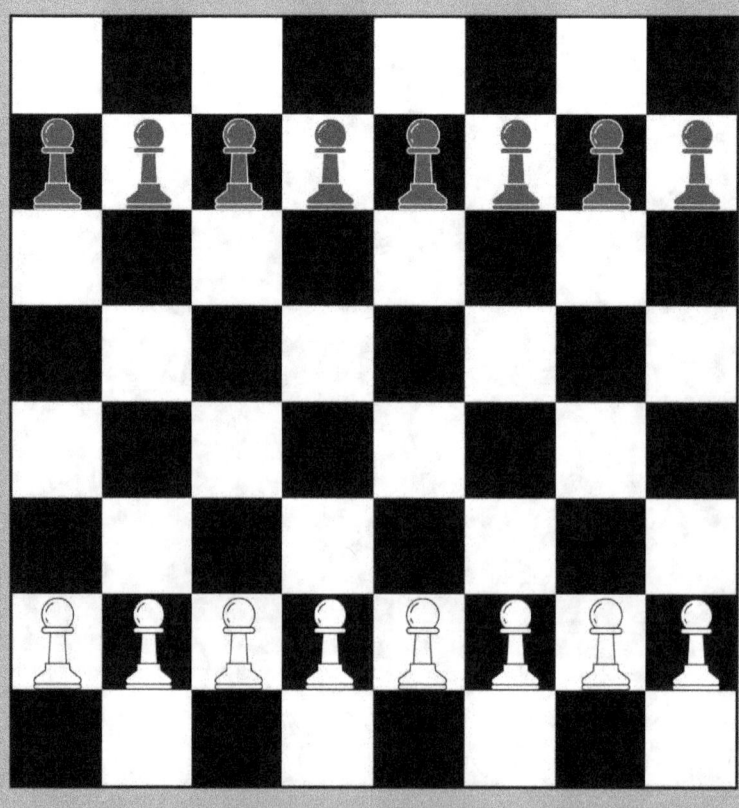

ROOK

- **Each player has 2 rooks.**
- **They are placed in the first row, one in each corner as shown in the image.**

BISHOP

- Each player has 2 bishops.
- They are placed on the first row.
- You have to place one between the knight and the queen and another between the king and the knight.

KNIGHT

- **Each player has 2 knights.**
- **They are placed on the first row.**
- **Each knight is placed between the rook and the bishop.**

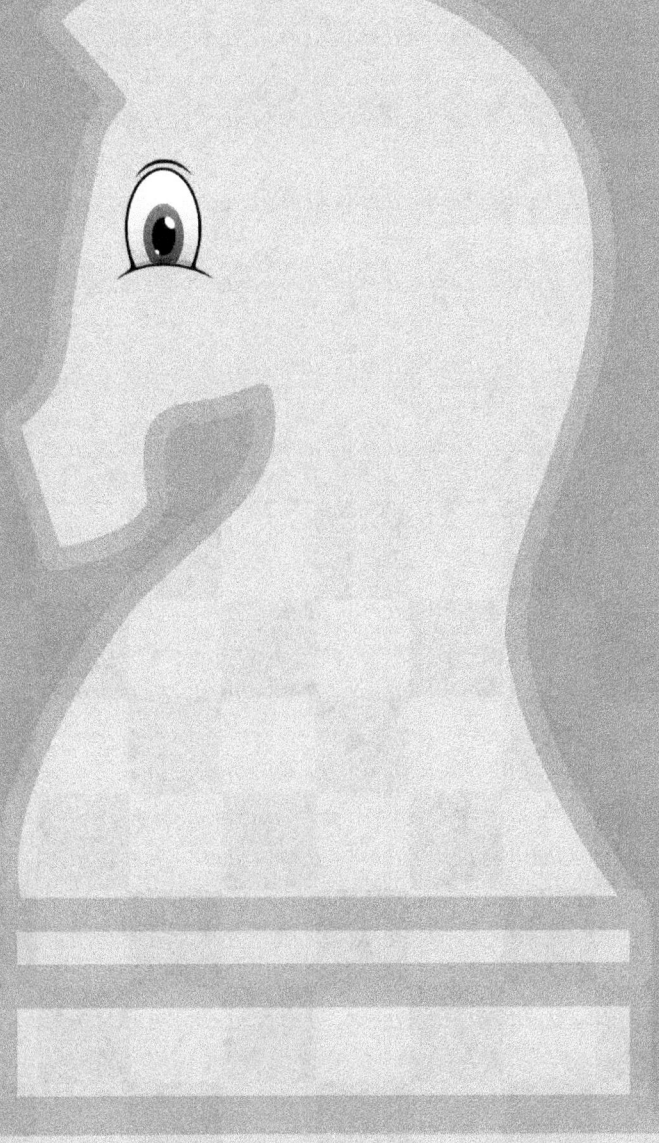

QUEEN

- **Each player has 1 queen.**
- **It is placed on the first row.**
- **The queen is placed between the bishop and the king.**

KING

- Each player has 1 king.
- It is placed on the first row.
- It is placed between the queen and the bishop.

2. How to move the pieces

- PAWN
- ROOK
- BISHOP
- KNIGHT
- QUEEN
- KING

PAWN

- Yellow dots show the possible moves which a pawn can make from its current position.
- It moves forward just one square at a time.
- On its first move, it can move up to two squares forward.
- It can't go backwards.
- It can take a rival's piece if it is on a diagonal square in front of the pawn as you can see in the picture (the white pawn could capture the black pawn piece). It can't move to a diagonal square if it's empty.
- It has two special moves: promotion and passant.

ROOK

- Yellow dots show the possible moves which a rook can make from its current position.
- It can move as much as you want across the board.
- It can move only one direction at a time.
- It can only move by rows, horizontal or vertical (not diagonally).

BISHOP

- Yellow dots show the possible moves which a bishop can make from its current position.
- It moves diagonally, either on the white squares or on the black squares.
- It can move as many squares as you like in one turn.
- It can only move once per turn.

KNIGHT

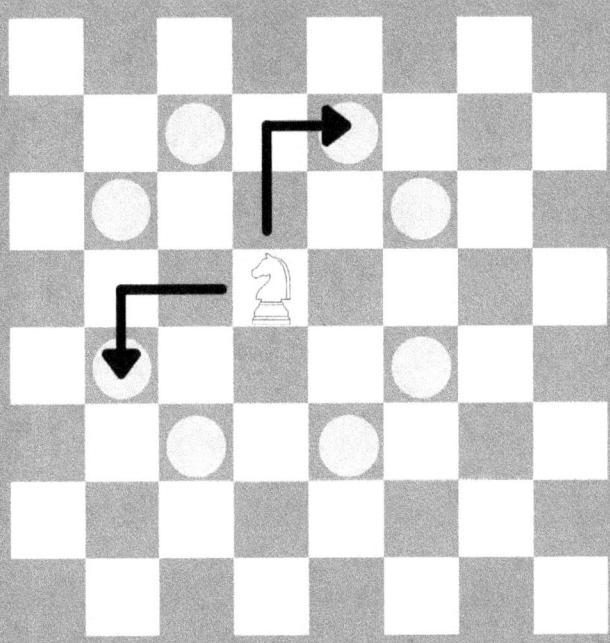

- Yellow dots show the possible moves which a knight can make from its current position.
- It moves like an "L": 2 horizontal or vertical squares and 1 perpendicular square.
- The move ends on a different color than the one at the beginning.
- It can jump on top of whichever piece (your own or your rivals) in order to finish its move.
- You can capture a piece if it is placed on the last square where the knight goes.

QUEEN

- Yellow dots show the possible moves which a queen can make from its current position.
- It can move horizontal, vertical and diagonally, but only one direction at a time per turn.
- It can move as many squares as you like at a time.

KING

- Yellow dots show the possible moves which a king can make from its current position.
- It can move in all directions, but one square at a time.
- It can't take a piece if there is another one defending it.
- Its special move is "Castling", on which the king moves to the side of the rook, only if it is its first move and the square is vacant and not threatened by the rival.
- A king can't checkmate another king.

3. Elements

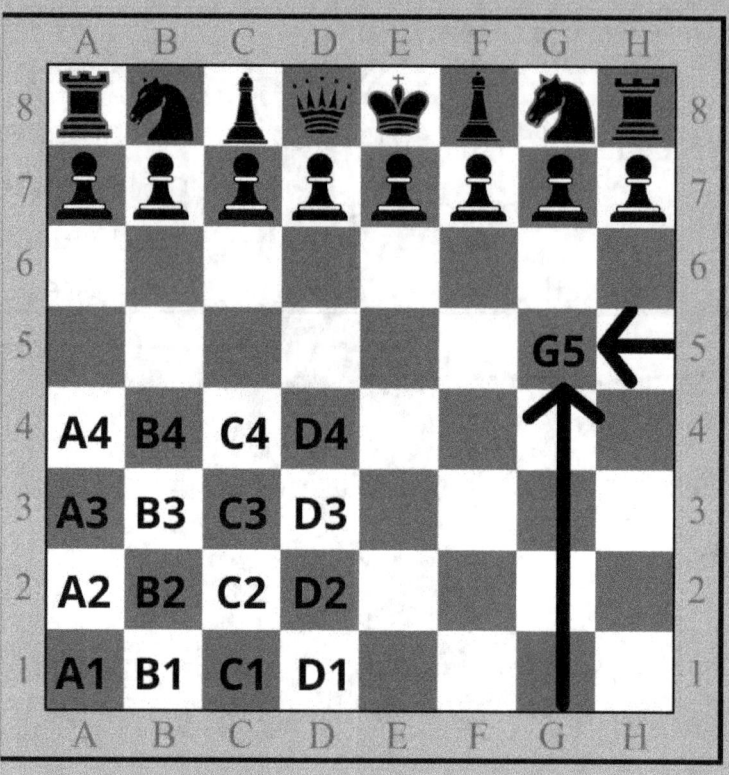

4. Special moves

CASTLING

It is a special move in which the king and the rook move at the same time.

You can only use Castling if:

- The king and the rook haven't moved at all.

- There is no piece between the king and the rook.

- The king is not on check.

- At the end of the move, the king doesn't end up on a square threatened by an opponent's piece.

Short castling

The king moves 2 squares to the right and the right rook moves 2 squares to the left as you can see shown on the picture.

Long castling

The left rook moves 3 squares to the right and the king moves 2 squares to the left, as you can see shown on the picture.

PASSANT

If a pawn, in its first move, moves 2 squares forward and ends up next to a rival's pawn, this rival pawn can capture it, as if it has only moved one square. The winner pawn would have to take place on the diagonal square.

This is a move that's only valid if it's played right after the pawn has moved the two squares forward.

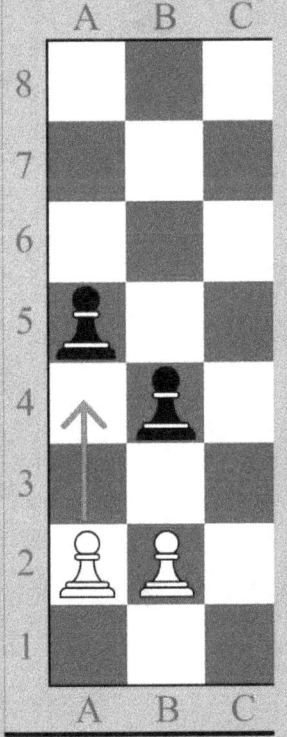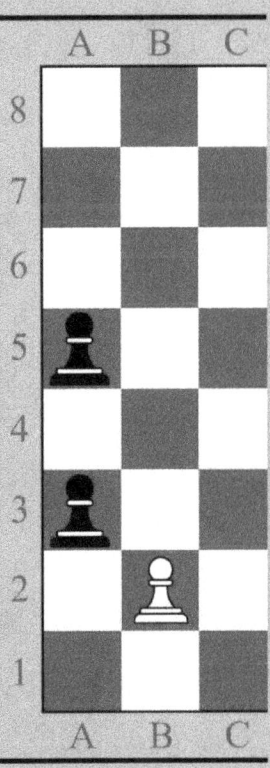

PROMOTION

If the pawn moves across the board up to the other end, then that piece can be promoted to a better one with greater value and power.

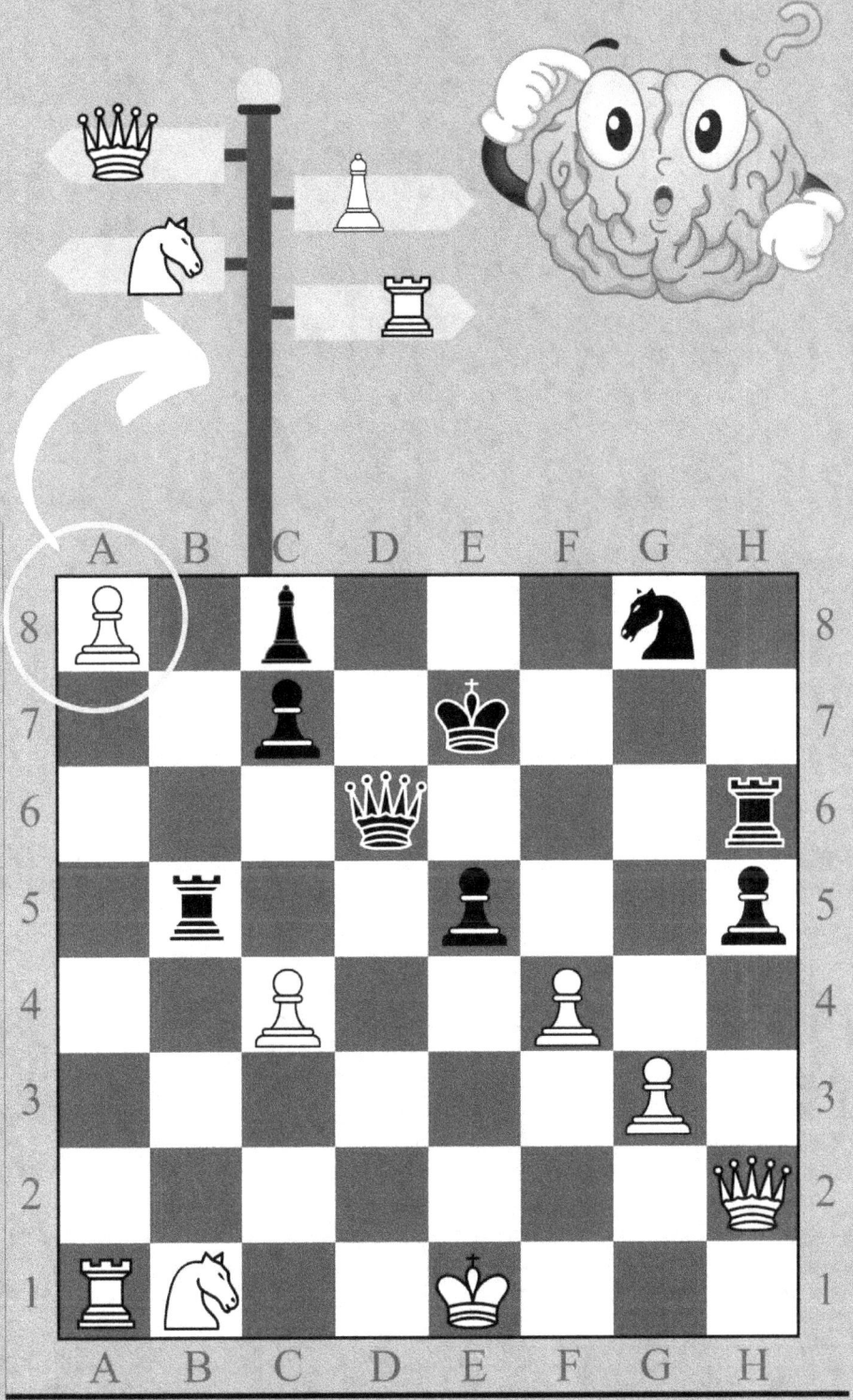

CHECK

Check is when the king or queen of one of the players is threatened to be captured on the next turn by a rival's piece.

If there is no way out for the king piece, then it's a Checkmate and the game is over. Some of the ways to get out of a "Check" are:

- Move the king to a non threatened square.
- Capture the piece the king is threatened by.
- Block the check by placing another piece in between.

Possibles ways out of a Check

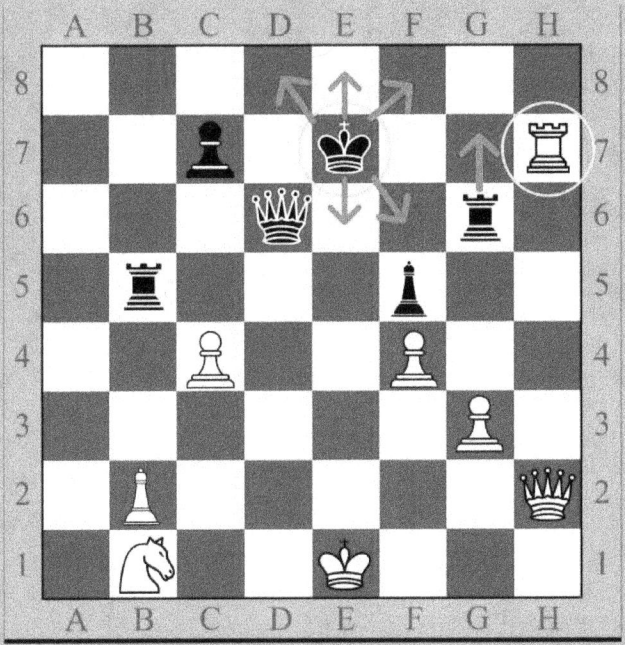

Checkmate example

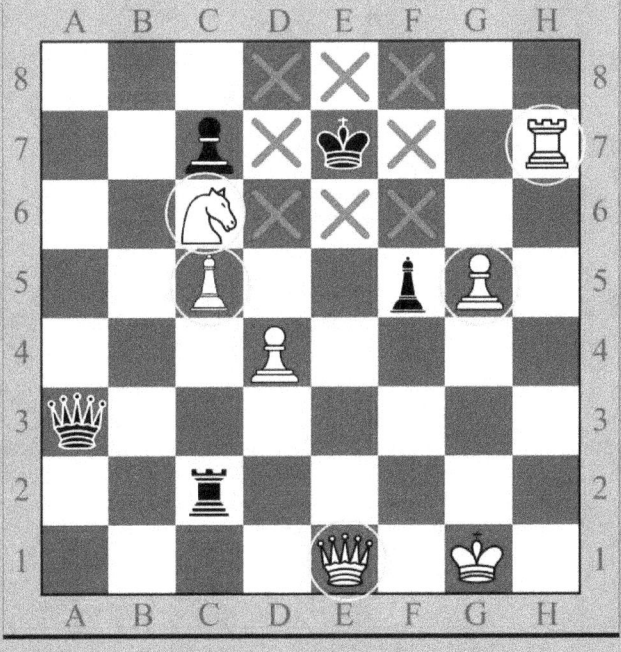

5. Some rules

- The player with white pieces goes first.

- No piece can jump over other pieces except the knight.

- Each player can only move one piece at a time. "Castling" move is an exception.

- If there is a square occupied by your own piece, it can't be replaced by another one of our pieces. It is only possible to occupy a square where our rival has a piece on it, which is better known as "capturing or taking" the piece.

The king can't be captured. If the king is threatened to be captured on the next turn, it's called a "check" and the king at risk must protect itself on its next move or be protected by another piece. If this is not a possibility, then it is checkmate and the owner of the threatened king loses the game.

- All pieces can move backwards except pawns.

- Every player must move a piece on their turn to play.

6. End of game

a) Checkmate

Unlike the rest of the pieces, the king is the only one that can't be captured. If the rival can take the king on the next turn and there is no way out, then the game is over.

b) Quitting the game

Any player could quit the game at any point, so the winner would be the opponent who doesn't quit.

c) Draw or tie

The game can end as a draw or tie under these conditions:

- If none of the kings is in check but both players don't have any possible move available for next turn, the case is called "drowned king".

- If neither player can't get to a checkmate position due to the nature of the remaining pieces. For example: king vs king, king vs king and bishop, king vs king and knight, king and bishop vs king and bishop.

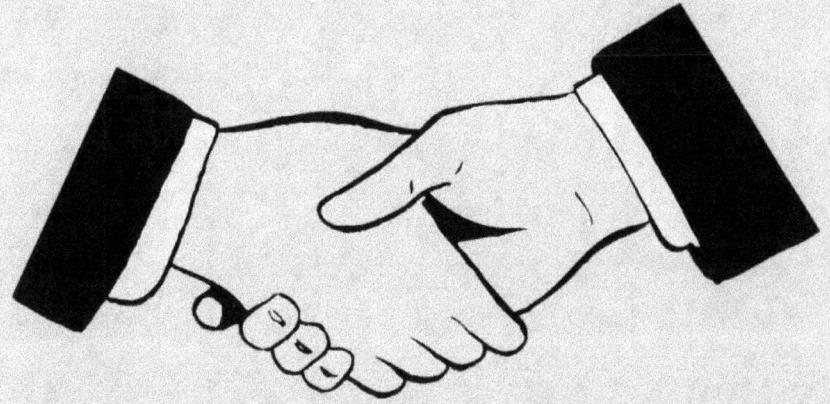

- If the players agree to Draw.

d) Waste of time

If the game is played under time conditions, the game could end when one of the players uses all the time he/she has. Players can have a certain amount of time or a number of moves they can make on a certain term.

This is all for now...

If you liked it, please, leave me a review on the website where you bought it, it just will take you a minute or less and it would mean the world to me.

I really appreciate you taking the time to read and review this book.

Good luck in your battles!!

I have more books for you!!

www.ingramcontent.com/pod-product-compliance
Lightning Source LLC
Chambersburg PA
CBHW071146060526
44107CB00132B/248